Expansive Prayer

Expansive Prayer

Reflections for All Seasons

Philip A. Verhalen

Paulist Press
New York/Mahwah, N.J.

Cover and book design by Lynn Else

Library of Congress Cataloging-in-Publication Data

Verhalen, Philip A.
    Expansive prayer : reflections for all seasons / Philip A. Verhalen.
        p. cm.
    Includes bibliographical references.
    ISBN 0-8091-4213-9 (alk. paper)
    1. Meditations. 2. Catholic Church—Prayer-books and devotions—English.
I. Title.

    BX2182.3.V47 2004
    242—dc22

                                                        2003028125

Published by Paulist Press
997 Macarthur Boulevard
Mahwah, New Jersey 07430

www.paulistpress.com

Printed and bound in the
United States of America

Contents

Acknowledgments vii

Author's Note ix

Fall 1

    The Vineyard 3

    Fog 7

    Coming Down from the Mountain 10

    Anxiety and Hope 14

    Thanksgiving 21

Winter 23

    The Unjust Judge 25

    Christmas 28

    The Anointing at Bethany
      or The Second-to-Last Supper 32

    Erase and Repent 38

Spring 41

    The April Fool—Jesus Christ 43

    Service and Leadership 50

    The Eucharist 54

    Good and Evil 58

Contents

Summer 61

      Forgiveness 63

      God the Communicator 66

      Authentic Personhood 72

      Faith, Tradition, and Love 75

Notes 79

A Brief Book List on Prayer 81

Acknowledgments

I wish to thank the editors of Paulist Press for their warm support in bringing this book to completion. Especially, I thank Elizabeth Walter, Paul McMahon, Kevin di Camillo, and Father Lawrence Boadt. Their steady sensitivity and technical expertise have provided an atmosphere of ease that every writer craves.

If it takes a village to raise a child, it takes a global village to inspire a book. A precious panoply of talent, creativity, awareness, human encouragement, honest criticism, and sustaining love have provided the solid impetus I needed to pursue this project. I thank all of these remarkable and delightful friends. Especially do I thank: John Foster, SJ; Dorothy and Phil Brandt; Tim Milnes; John Olivier; Bob and Helen Batie; Walt and Margie Babb; Walt and Donna Abel; Chris Gavin; Jack Peterson; Rita Kowats; Jim Goodwin, SJ; Ray and Marian Malonson; Ibar Lynch; Dale Turner; my brothers Charlie and Jim, and Flo, Jim's wonderful wife; my dear sister, Rosie; her son Ed Cummings and his wife Erin; and many others at Bellarmine Prep in Tacoma. Moreover, I wish to thank Fred and Polly at TypeRight for placing this text in an attractive and orderly form. To all of you my affection and thanks.

Dedication

To My Family
Charlie, Jim and Flo, Rosie and Joe (R.I.P)

Always There
Always Care

Author's Note

Every two weeks at Bellarmine Prep, the faculty and staff come together for prayer and reflection, in addition to our weekly eucharistic liturgy and our daily prayers in the classroom. We as a faculty and staff consider our prayer time together uniquely significant.

Bellarmine is a rather close-knit community. Friendships among our families go back beyond twenty years in many cases. We pray in a familial manner. We choose themes that are often delicate and risky. We take turns leading these prayer events. This custom goes back more than thirty years under the warm leadership of the Jesuit Fathers, who founded this school in 1928.

The meditative reflections in this book contain many of the prayers I used for these spiritual encounters. Some of the reflections are drawn from other occasions, but most date back to those early-morning experiences in the school chapel when all of us gathered together before God to ask for insight and renewed strength for a work that all of us consider to be most engaging under God's direction.

Philip A. Verhalen
Tacoma, Washington
December 2002

FALL

The Vineyard

I want to invite you to a scene in New Testament times, two-thousand years ago. The scene more properly is called a parable, which leads easily to an allegory. Perhaps we can call on our imagination to provide the setting for a parable.

The Scene

Imagine you are in a small village square around noon time on a very hot fall day. A few men are gathered at the cantina under the cover of a lattice work threaded with vines.

It is harvest time. And the talk is all about the promise of an abundant wine harvest. Some of the recent cool nights have brought the grapes to the point where they must be picked... now...today, if possible.

Two rather old men have taken up a conversation with a young worker who is new to these parts. The young man has no work. He hopes to find work by waiting around the marketplace. He heard that there is a certain landowner who comes to the marketplace frequently when he has need of workers.

The young man is hopeful for work today. He looks around the square. He sees other men, idle, not working. Perhaps other men need work as much as he does.

The two older men recall some of the stories of the village and volunteer to tell them to the young man hopeful of employment. One of the older men, in a reflective mood, remembers a story Jesus told when he was preaching in the area. In this story, Jesus makes a comparison between this man's needs and the goals of the Jews looking toward the kingdom of God. He says:

3

"Now the kingdom of heaven is like a landowner going out at daybreak to hire workers for his vineyard. He made an agreement with the workers for one denarius a day, and sent them to his vineyard. Going out at about the third hour he saw others standing idle in the marketplace and said to them, 'You go to my vineyard too and I will give you a fair wage.' So they went. At about the sixth hour and again at about the ninth hour, he went out and did the same. Then at about the eleventh hour he went out and found more men standing round, and he said to them, 'Why have you been standing here idle all day?' 'Because no one has hired us' they answered. He said to them, 'You go into my vineyard too.' In the evening, the owner of the vineyard said to his bailiff, 'Call the workers and pay them their wages, starting with the last arrivals and ending with the first.' So those who were hired at about the eleventh hour came forward and received one denarius each. When the first came, they expected to get more, but they too received one denarius each. They took it, but grumbled at the landowner. 'The men who came last' they said 'have done only one hour, and you have treated them the same as us, though we have done a heavy day's work in all the heat.' He answered one of them and said, 'My friend, I am not being unjust to you; did we not agree on one denarius? Take your earnings and go. I choose to pay the last-comer as much as I pay you. Have I no right to do what I like with my own? Why be envious because I am generous?' Thus the last will be first, and the first, last."[1]

(Matt 20:1-16)

Reflection

With the pace and mood of the village storyteller, let us reflect this morning on the landowner as our divine Father who calls us to his vineyard.

We are told that a denarius was a day's wages in the time of this Gospel parable. It was fair, but not especially generous. Let us imagine that God hires each of us into the harvest of life. He calls us at different times and under different circumstances. Yet, with a certain strange urgency, he calls all of us now to the same place. Called after the Jews, most of us might consider ourselves late-comers. Whatever the time that we come into the vineyard, God promises us a fair wage...no details...no special math...a fair wage.

We work hard; some of us from the first hour...many of us from the third and sixth hours. The sun is hot and the work is hard. By the end of the day we feel that we have had a workout—a real workout. God's plans are strange. He sends workers into the vineyard even one brief hour before quitting time. Why? What can they possibly accomplish? *Ahhhh*...quitting time.

I get paid. Let's see, I came at the first hour. I will get a denarius. I watch the paymaster pay the eleventh-hour crew first. Well! *They* get a denarius. Amazing! The master might give me six or seven on that basis. It's my turn. I get but one denarius. I turn to my friend Joatham. He came at the first hour also. He gets one denarius. Oh?

The words roll out...not polite words, not gracious. What kind of a landowner is this? What is his fairness ethic for our lives?

At that point the landowner walks over and looks straight at me. His eyes are clear and honest, penetratingly honest, but now they frighten me to a slight degree. He says, "My friend"...a boss calling me a friend. He is disarming me. He continues: "I am not being unjust to you. Did we not agree on one denarius?...Take your earnings...I choose to pay the latecomer as much as you. Have I no right? Why be envious because I am generous? The last will be first..."

Prayer

O God, help me to understand your generosity. Like you, your love and graciousness are not always clear, and do not fit with my earthbound standards. I am used to measuring. But, with you, there is no suitable yardstick.

I am not pleased when people who work less than I do fall into the same or even greater fortune. I dislike working hard and long hours. And no one seems to recognize my work. By your actions *you* do not seem to acknowledge my hard work. How do I come to understand that you are generous to me when you are so very generous to others who work so little?

Or do they work so little? Those eleventh hour workers! What are you telling me, God?

My relationship with you is special, personal. You regard no other human being quite the same way. How do I know? You told me through the years that each human being is unique.

You give me many gifts: gifts at birth, gifts throughout life, gifts as I work—unique gifts. Now I want to measure your love, and I make a fatal mistake. I turn to my neighbor, who came into your vineyard at another time, under different circumstances. I compare myself with him or her, yet my neighbor is a worker with different gifts..

Why is it I will not accept your generosity to others? Is it not a certain blindness called envy?

O God, help me not to shortchange your love and generosity by looking at my neighbor and by trying to make a measurable comparison.

O God, let me give glory and praise to you for creating unique human persons. Never in your plan will there be dullness, tedium, or boredom. We are all so different. Keep me from measuring the stages of life in time (first or eleventh hour), or space (this work or that work). Let me live with the mystery of your love and generosity. Let me grow to appreciate it.

Fog

As a college student I did not particularly look forward to the start of another school year. However, I anticipated quite eagerly our annual outing just before the fall term. Each year a group of us male students would take a week's vacation at Clark Lake in Door County, Wisconsin. One of my friend's parents owned a cabin on the lake, well suited for a small group of college boys needing to relax before the rigors of studies assailed them. The time together was great fun!

One morning, a particularly foggy morning about 7:00 a.m., two of the fisherman "types" in our group announced that they were going fishing. Would any of us care to join them? Well rested, but lacking in imagination to do otherwise, I decided to join them. By the time we got into the rowboat, we had become a party of five, two anglers and three strangers to the sport of fishing.

But how were we to find their favorite fishing spot in this fog? We decided to follow the shore, surveying each of the piers until we located one significant pier, then turn straight out into the deep for one hundred yards. There we would find the abundant trove of healthy hungry fish. What a plan!

I, the most nearsighted of all, kept to the bow, guarding the anchor. The skilled fishermen directed the craft and identified the piers as we rowed slowly along the shore.

At the appointed pier, we turned out into the pea-soup fog, moving slowly as we counted off the yards. The whole experience caused us to talk wildly to each other about the folly of this endeavor. One said, "Don't we have anything better to do?" We all laughed uproariously. When we arrived at the predetermined spot, I was told to drop anchor.

Since I hadn't had too much responsibility during this entire outing, I took my newfound duties seriously. I lifted the iron anchor above my shoulders and, as if in Olympic style, spun the anchor two full circles before I threw it out into the deep. "Ka splash," loud and clear. I believe I made an impression on the fish!

We all laughed. We were decidedly anchored in about fifteen feet of water. So we—that is, the fishermen—began to fish. The rest of us chatted and laughed, and bantered about everything we could think of in the midst of this new and quite pleasant venture.

The fog was so thick we could barely see beyond the gunnels of our boat. So what? We were having fun. Eventually we quieted down. That pleased the serious fishermen in the group.

Time moved slowly. The boat was small, the fog was thick, and three of us lacked the patience that accompanies a true fisherman's spirit. Slowly the fog lifted. We began to see the sky and the water as distinct. We saw color. Then eventually the fog lifted completely. And guess what? We found ourselves in an arena of boats—smack dab in the middle, all around us, fishermen in serious posture, poles and lines extended. Well! I was surprised, then embarrassed. My goodness! I had believed that we were all alone in the middle of a big lake. I thought, "Let's get out of here." I was too embarrassed to stay in this coterie of serious fishermen. I was out of place, way out! Speaking softly now, I asked the other four if it would be okay to leave. Strangely, they all agreed. Sheepishly I drew up the anchor, and we went back to our cabin.

Reflection

Sometimes we are in a fog. We know it, but we think we are all alone in this unusual experience. In this personal story I retold, everybody outside our own group was in a fog also, but they knew how to deal with it. They knew how to fish in spite of the fog.

Another word comes to mind, a synonym for fog, namely—mystery. Sometimes I am sitting in a meeting wondering what is going on. I am perplexed, but it appears that I alone experience this perplexity. Then someone speaks, sharing his puzzlement. Eventually others chime in. We all are in a fog. We simply deal with it differently.

I believe life is a mystery. We only find out a few things about life before we die. The rest is mystery. Can I continue to fish quietly in the fog? Do I need to yell out to attract attention? Should I stop fishing and pull up anchor?

I believe that God guides us ever so gently to our "fishing spot." We can feel all alone in the fog, but that is untrue. Many of us are there in the same spot, doing the best we can to catch fish. Depending on our past experience and developed skills, some of us deal with this fog called mystery quite well. Others do not.

The mystery of life, like the fog, does not always lift with the daytime sun. We simply might be in a place where there is a great deal of fog most of the year.

I am thinking of the West Coast of the United States near the mouth of the Columbia. The fog sits comfortably along the coast throughout the long winter months. The residents live there with an intuitive understanding of the fog as part of their lives. They live there for many reasons, such as a calm lifestyle, pleasant surroundings, gracious neighbors, an opportunity to be fully alive and to do the things that enrich their lives. The fog interferes with none of this. The fog is an integral part of their chosen atmosphere for living.

I hope that I can live with the mystery of my life with the same calm that these residents of the West Coast live with their fog.

Mystery still challenges me. But soon I hope to become so accepting of it that I begin to cherish mystery as a dear friend. The challenge remains but evolves. The mystery, like fog, is part of the air—the hydrogen, the oxygen. I cannot expect to live without it. My life, my breath, my spirit are all of a whole. The mystery of my life is part of what defines my personhood. Hmmm! Am I getting used to this fog?

Coming Down
from the Mountain

In this meditation, I wish to appeal to both our intellect and our imagination as we speak to our God.

First, let us imagine we are alone and moving slowly, deliberately, up a beautiful mountain trail in the middle of Idaho. The day is cool, with a brilliant sun giving direct warmth to our face as we turn upward along the path.

We proceed slowly but steadily. Let us imagine that Jesus is at the top of the mountain. He will join us as we pray and review our personal faith in the Almighty God of Abraham, Isaac, and Jacob. He will help us to open ourselves to the Spirit that speaks within us.

We have reached the top of this rugged mountain. A soft wind greets us, evoking a feeling of peace and quiet that triggers our memory of past experiences of such remarkable tranquillity.

We are becoming more and more calm. We are relaxed. We listen to our breathing—still heaving from the hike along the trail. In and out...our chest moves deliberately, but more easily, and the rhythm becomes more regular and comfortable.

We begin to feel at one with our God, as close as can be. We do not see God, but we sense he is there.

We pick up the Scriptures and read of another time, but two thousand years ago, when Jesus was coming down from a mountain, not unlike this one in Idaho. Jesus has been transfigured before his closest friends, his apostles Peter, James, and John.

At that point he needed and received the consolation of being close to his father. He came down the mountain and felt himself back in the usual, fast-paced world...with its struggles and conflicts all waiting to be resolved.

In Mark we read:

When they rejoined the disciples they saw a large crowd round them and some scribes arguing with them. The moment they saw him the whole crowd were struck with amazement and ran to greet him. "What are you arguing about with them?" he asked. A man answered him from the crowd, "Master, I have brought my son to you; there is a spirit of dumbness in him, and when it takes hold of him it throws him to the ground, and he foams at the mouth and grinds his teeth and goes rigid. And I asked your disciples to cast it out and they were unable to." "You faithless generation," he said to them in reply. "How much longer must I be with you? How much longer must I put up with you? Bring him to me." They brought the boy to him, and as soon as the spirit saw Jesus it threw the boy into convulsions, and he fell to the ground and lay writhing there, foaming at the mouth. Jesus asked the father, "How long has this been happening to him?" "From childhood," he replied. "And it has often thrown him into the fire and into the water, in order to destroy him. But if you can do anything, have pity on us and help us." "If you can?" retorted Jesus. "Everything is possible for anyone who has faith." Immediately the father of the boy cried out, "I do have faith. Help the little faith I have!" And when Jesus saw how many people were pressing round him, he rebuked the unclean spirit. "Deaf and dumb spirit," he said. "I command you: come out of him and never enter him again." Then throwing the boy into violent convulsions it came out shouting, and the boy lay there so like a corpse that most of them said, "He is dead." But Jesus took him by the hand and helped him up, and he was able to stand. When he had

11

gone indoors his disciples asked him privately, "Why were we unable to cast it out?" "This is the kind," he answered, "that can only be driven out by prayer."

(Mark 9:14–29)

Reflection

O Jesus, each of us comes privately to you and says: "Why can I not root out pain, affliction, suffering, mental anguish, and physical maladies?"

You say to the apostles, "You must pray," and to the father of the epileptic son, "Everything is possible for one who has faith." O Lord...I have faith, but give me more faith.

...Not faith that will move mountains...but faith that will move me, and my family, and my friends.

...Not move me to the unusual or miraculous, but move me to sense your power, your life coursing through my veins and arteries...to the very tips of my fingers and toes.

O Lord, I have faith, but faith is like a muscle. It needs routine exercise; it requires activity on a daily basis. Its exercise must be a habit if it is to be part of my life.

O Lord, help me cultivate the habit of faith...although this faith may not be the strongest...it is, nevertheless, alive and struggling and growing.

In the Letter to the Hebrews, I read—

Only faith can guarantee the blessings that we hope for, or prove the existence of the realities that at present remain unseen. It was for faith that our ancestors were commended.

It is by faith that we understand that the world was created by one word from God, so that no apparent cause can account for the things we can see.

(Heb 11:1–3)

We see so much, yet understand so little. Should that surprise us? Then follows an account of so many Old Testament personalities exhibiting faith.

For example, Abraham is discussed in this same letter:

It was by faith that Abraham obeyed the call to set out for a country that was the inheritance given to him and his descendants, and that he set out without knowing where he was going. By faith he arrived, as a foreigner, in the Promised Land, and lived there as if in a strange country, with Isaac and Jacob, who were heirs with him of the same promise. They lived there in tents while he looked forward to a city founded, designed and built by God.

(Heb 11:8–10)

O Lord, we live in tents, but we look forward to living in a city founded, designed, and built by God, your Father, our sovereign Lord. *Glory be to the Father, and to the Son, and to the Holy Spirit, as it was in the beginning, is now and ever shall be, world without end...Amen.*

Anxiety and Hope

Introduction

Consider Beethoven's 8th Sonata, a brilliant example of his genius before he became deaf. Beethoven assists us in our understanding of the difference between fear and anxiety, the two ideas incorporated in our meditation today. Beethoven did not fear death, but he experienced keen anxiety about his problems of living, from deafness, to poverty, to a variety of other insecurities. For years he felt ostracized from society because of his deafness, but he never gave up courage.

Paul Tillich is someone we will call on later for our meditation. His book *The Courage to Be*[2] is the basis for the central theme of this reflection.

Reflection

Let us reflect upon the presence of God who connects us to life—its way, its truth, and its reality.

Let us begin with a setting so natural, yet so extraordinary, we will remember it as a place of special peace and refreshment.

There are many settings we could choose; for our meditation this morning, let us choose a cliff in the Northwest, overlooking the Pacific Ocean.

Let us imagine that we have walked out to the crest of a rocky ledge overlooking a deep chasm among a series of overhanging rocks. We place ourselves comfortably on a blanket, resting our arms on our knees. We look out over the vast expanse of the blue Pacific, then draw our eyes once again to our immediate surroundings as we listen to the roar of the waves against the rocky ridges standing as bold sentinels facing the rigors of wind and sea.

We pick up the rhythm of the constant beating and swirling of the waters caught in the small bays and chasms of the serrated landscape.

Marianne Moore, in her poem "What Are Years," sets the scene, the tone, and the theme of our reflections this morning. She says:

> He sees deep and is glad, who
>   accedes to mortality
> and in his imprisonment, rises
> upon himself as
> the sea in a chasm, struggling to be
> free and unable to be,
>   in its surrendering
>   finds its continuing.[3]

First, let us reflect on our mortality. We begin Lent with the declaration of Ash Wednesday: "Remember, man, that you are dust, and unto dust you shall return."[4] What it really says is: At one time we were nothing. Then we came to life here on earth, however brief a time, then we die, and, in cold philosophical language, we return to non-being.

A simple look at this cycle creates anxiety in our lives, an anxiety that can never be quite eradicated. Paul Tillich speaks of this anxiety in a book called *The Courage to Be*. The title itself indicates the solution for this anxiety. It is courage tied to the virtues of faith, hope, and love.

In this book, Tillich makes a practical but revealing distinction. He tells us that in life two things wear upon us: our fears and our anxiety. These two conditions can be so overwhelming that we hardly note the distinction. However, for our spiritual and mental health, it seems fitting that we become aware of this distinction.

Let us begin with the idea of fear. Fear always has an object. For example: fear of crowds, fear of tests, fear of heights, fear of water, fear of math teachers. Because these fears have an object, we can deal with them by looking at the object. Outside support is readily available to help us deal with our fears. Then, as we progress through life, we try to reach that state of serenity whereby we have no more fears. We grow to become afraid of nothing.

Anxiety is a different issue—it has no object. Anxiety is built directly into our lives as humans. We are anxious because it is the human condition. This anxiety becomes yet more compelling as we grow older. Our "angst" (German), or anxiety, basically tells us we come from nothing and will return to nothing. Remember, mankind, you are dust and unto dust you shall return. We must learn to deal with "the space between" as swiftly passing time.

The anxiety of life flows through the themes of Hebrew Scriptures like slowly moving molasses. We find this inexorable movement particularly in the Wisdom literature. Almost imperceptibly it grows with the changing Jewish culture of the three or four centuries before the Christian era. Let me mention some few examples of this Jewish awareness of anxiety:

"Look, you have given me an inch or two of life,
my life span is nothing to you;
each man that stands on earth is only a puff of wind,
every man that walks, only a shadow...." (Ps 39:5-6)

or

"Swifter than a weaver's shuttle my days have passed,
and vanished, leaving no hope behind.
Remember that my life is but a breath..." (Job 7:6-7)

and the remarkable beginning of Ecclesiastes: "Vanity of vanities, Qoheleth says. Vanity of vanities. All is vanity. For all his toil, his toil under the sun, what does man gain by it?" (1:2-3).

Qoheleth was woefully distressed about his condition, once he identified his anxiety (or angst). In our own time this anxiety lingers vividly in the poet's memory. For example, Ernest Dawson, who lived only to the age of 32, experienced a brief and luckless career of sipping wine and flinging roses at the world. He laments searchingly:

They are not long, the days of wine and roses:
Out of a misty dream
Our path emerges for a while, then closes
within a dream.[5]

Strangely enough, we find ourselves understanding the plight of our fellow humans down through the centuries. Moreover, lest we become discouraged by our own anxiety, Tillich directs us to be the model of Jesus the Messiah and asks us to develop the *courage to be*. In other words, he asks us to reaffirm the present moment as that which is most significant in our lives. Jesus urges us not to worry about the past, nor to worry about the future, but to look to the present and its hope of being in the reality of the moment itself.

Christ draws us to understand our own need for courage as members of a larger community that shares all sorts of experiences. We all know what it means to reach out for courage, to seize it, and to hold it with the hope-filled strength of every fiber of our being.

As Christians, we spontaneously turn to Christ, a human person who understood the challenges of life. His Spirit sustains us and helps us to realize that our life on this planet earth, however brief, is a study in acceptance: First, that we are mortal; and second, that we recognize in this mortality the value of courage to seek out the meaning of our day-to-day existence, however mundane it may seem.

We sit on this ledge and look down at the sea, and we realize once more the power of Marianne Moore's words:

He sees deep and is glad, who
accedes to mortality
and in his imprisonment, rises
upon himself as
the sea in a chasm, struggling to be
free and unable to be,
in its surrendering
finds its continuing.

The consolation in this poem rests in the words: "in its sur-
rendering/finds it continuing."

Mysteriously, God gives us the gift to find the meaning of life
in our surrender, somewhat inexplicably, but nonetheless hopefully.

The continuing ebb and flow of life's experiences somehow
hold the answer to the mystery of our own personal lives given to
us by God.

Once we realize that we are imprisoned by our mortality, we
might wonder if a certain fatalistic logic will overcome us.

We ask: "Why not join the theater of the absurd?" as if in frustration that whatever we do today will be of little consequence by
the time we come to the end of our lives.

So we ask further: *"Cui bono?"* What good is it? What good is
it to struggle in this world to give assistance to our fellow humans?
We are all going to die one day. We are finite; we will never do very
much in one brief lifetime. Should we not simply relax and wait for
death to overtake us? Reinhold Niebuhr gives us a response to this
line of questioning by drawing us to the Christian virtues of faith,
hope, and love. He simply says:

"What Saves Us? Nothing that is worth doing can be
achieved in our lifetime; therefore we must be saved by
hope. Nothing which is true or beautiful or good makes
complete sense in any immediate context of history; therefore we must be saved by faith. Nothing we do, however

virtuous, can be accomplished alone; therefore we are saved by love."[6]

As I look out over the ledge at the sea swirling below, I slowly reflect:

in its surrendering, finds its continuing.

Other people lead us to eternity in spite of our mortality, supporting this idea of surrender.

We must somehow admit to the limits of being finite, of being tied to time and space. Imprisoned in time and space with Marianne Moore, we see our life as "the sea in a chasm, struggling to be free and unable to be."

To live day in and day out with some purpose and meaning requires a courage that reaffirms life daily as we venture forward, facing the challenges of this existence. We live with a built-in anxiety about our finite condition, but in Christ we live with hope about the future.

Moreover, there exists an ongoing puzzlement about our very dignity. The dignity of finite living blooms outward in the words of Walt Whitman:

I know I am august
I do not trouble my spirit to vindicate itself

or to be understood,
I see the elementary laws never apologize,
(I reckon I behave no prouder than
the level I plant my house by after all.)

I exist as I am, that is enough,
If no other in the world be aware I sit content
And if each and all be aware I sit content.[7]

Whitman affirms life in its natural setting. He understands life from its surroundings: life that is finite, that is limited; life that has value as limited in its very setting.

in its surrendering, finds its continuing.

Tillich rightfully distinguishes fear as tied to some object, and anxiety as an essential part of the human finite condition.

We may or may not fear the event of death, but dealing with all the limits of life that end up in non-being, in other words death, causes anxiety. From moment-to-moment we realize that we are finite and can only reach out so far in our thoughts or actions.

We sit on this rocky cliff and we think of another time and place. We envision Jesus sitting on the side of a hill, looking out over the Sea of Galilee. He faces the idea of anxiety under the aegis of worry. Jesus tells us not to worry about our lives, what we are to eat, how we are to be clothed. "Look at the birds of the sky. They do not sow or reap" (Matt 6:26). Obviously Christ expects us to be concerned about our duties as parents to provide food and clothing and shelter for our children, but concern is quite different from worry or undue anxiety.

"Remember, man, that you are dust, and unto dust you shall return."

We live out our anxiety in Lent with courage. We affirm each day with courage. We face the problems of life with courage. We promote integrity and justice, and love each day as if it were our last. And, you know, some day we will be correct.

So we leave the rocky ledge of this serene coastal region and return to our routine of daily work and rest in this brief season called life.

Thanksgiving

Introduction

The Pilgrims set the tone. Now each year we celebrate autumn in thankfulness. Unfortunately our change from an agricultural to an urban people has challenged this spirit of harvest gratitude. On separate occasions we might be prompted to say that Thanksgiving is all about football, while we still cherish our roots and hold to the romantic memory of visiting Grandma.

In this prayerful time, I would like to recall some motives for our thankfulness. We are decidedly a Judeo-Christian culture, but we also have Greco-Roman roots. In the classics, Seneca, Plutarch, and Cicero lead the way in telling us of the value of *gratitude*.[8]

Reflection

Seneca says: "He who urges gratitude pleads the cause both of God and men, for without it we can neither be sociable nor religious."

We learn our gratitude at home, from parents and elders. This experience both civilizes us culturally and personalizes us religiously. With a healthy spirit of gratitude we fit into the community, and eventually into the community of worship. I remember a student who was particularly irked that she needed to take a test the next day. When I handed her the test a brief twenty-four hours later, she replied, almost instinctively, "Thank you."

Plutarch says: "The worship most acceptable to God comes from a thankful and cheerful heart." Virtue and worship are intertwined from ancient to contemporary Christian times: we call our worship service *Eucharist*, which means *thanksgiving*.

Cicero calls gratitude the master of virtues, the most capital of all duties, and uses the words *grateful* and *good* as synonymous terms, inseparably united in the same character.

From David, our common Jewish ancestor, we learn to give thanks for everything. Jeremy Taylor adds: "Every furrow in the Book of Psalms is sown with the seeds of thanksgiving."

I would like to read a few parts of Psalm 107:

Give thanks to Yahweh, for he is good,
his love is everlasting:

Let these be the words of Yahweh's redeemed,
those he has redeemed from the oppressor's clutches,
by bringing them home from foreign countries,
from east and west, from north and south....

Let these thank Yahweh for his love,
for his marvels on behalf of men.
Let them offer thanksgiving sacrifices
and proclaim with shouts of joy what he has done.

(vv 1–3, 21–22)

Montaigne says: "There are few persons who publish to the world the prayers they make to almighty God." If this is true, you and I prefer a certain circumspection in our personal praying. Yet most of us are more comfortable with expressing our prayers of thanksgiving.

Izaac Walton says: "God has two dwellings, one in heaven and the other in a meek and thankful heart."

And in the words of Arthur Guiterman, we sing:

"So once in every year we throng upon a day apart,
To praise the Lord with feast and song,
In thankfulness of Heart."

WINTER

The Unjust Judge

The story of the unjust judge is quite simple, quite direct, but beneath the surface of this story lies much material for our spiritual growth.

Then he told them a parable about the need to pray continually and never lose heart. "There was a judge in a certain town," he said, "who had neither fear of God nor respect for man. In the same town there was a widow who kept on coming to him and saying, 'I want justice from you against my enemy!' For a long time he refused, but at last he said to himself, 'Maybe I have neither fear of God nor respect for man, but since she keeps pestering me I must give this widow her just rights, or she will persist in coming and worry me to death.'"

And the Lord said, "You notice what the unjust judge has to say? Now will not God see justice done to his chosen who cry to him day and night even when he delays to help them? I promise you, he will see justice done to them, and done speedily. But when the Son of Man comes, will he find any faith on earth?"

(Luke 18:1–9)

Reflection

Two ideas come immediately to mind. Jesus is asking us to pray and never give up praying. What is our reaction?

The parable contrasts the unjust judge with the just judge we call God.

The unjust judge has great power. He has power to decide and power to bring about solutions. However, he is not just in the use of his power.

He has wisdom, but it is "street" wisdom. He admittedly doesn't fear God or care about mankind.

Quite independent in his position of power, isn't he?

How does this parable give me an understanding of dealing with injustice in my life?

Often I feel:

"O God, I am bothering you."

"There is injustice in my life. How do I get justice?"

"Well, God, what are you doing about it?"

"How long must I wait? Where is your concern?"

"So God, are you not the Just Judge?"

"Give me justice before I tire you out!"

Or "God, are you different? The parable promises that you do give justice and quickly. How come I do not always perceive these promises in my life?"

Mystery hovers over this parable. I want justice, but God may have a different timetable. I am promised justice quickly, but God's life is not limited to time and space. How does God satisfy my own needs for justice, as I am reduced to living in time and space? Ah, the mystery.

One possible answer is tied to the beginning of the parable. Jesus says to pray always and not to give up praying.

Our life is to be a habit of praying, as it is a habit of breathing, and eating, and sleeping.

The punch line comes at the end in the form of a challenge. When the Son of God comes again, where is our faith? Will it be there, and be strong? So...Jesus says, always pray, don't give up.

Christmas

Talking to a close friend last year, I asked if he was getting ready for Christmas. He responded in his avuncular manner, befitting his eighty years: "Oh, Christmas is for children." At first I agreed, but then I raced ahead in my mind, thinking: "Yes, but are we not all meant to become children?" Christmas is a feast of the Christ Child, meant to be appreciated by all. We must get close to this newborn babe in spirit. I think that is the message the Gospel enjoins: "Unless you can become as little children, you cannot enter the kingdom of heaven" (Matt 18:2 and Luke 18:17).

At Christmas we begin the life of Jesus Christ liturgically. We tune into his life, become like him in his childhood, so we can attain the same childlike quality that qualifies us for his kingdom. So I guess now I would respond to the statement: "Christmas is for children" with "Yes, and that is the reason we all become children at Christmas time."

At Christmas we take out and put up our outdoor lights *one more time.*

We go out and select a tree, and decorate it *one more time.*

We bake those special Christmas cookies and invite the kids of the neighborhood to help us *one more time.*

We go shopping for those special presents *one more time.*

We wrap them and distribute them *one more time.*

We bring out the crib and set it up *one more time.*

Because at Christmas we must become as little children.

I am reminded what that means every time I recall the story of Sachi. Some of you may know this story. Let me recount it one more time.

Sachi

Soon after her brother was born, little Sachi began to ask her parents to leave her alone with the new baby. They worried that, like most four-year-olds, she might feel jealous and want to hit or shake him, so they said no. But she showed no signs of jealousy. She treated the baby with kindness and her pleas to be left alone with him became more urgent. They decided to allow it.

Elated, she went into the baby's room and shut the door, but it opened a crack—enough for her curious parents to peek in and listen. They saw little Sachi walk quietly up to her baby brother, put her face close to his, and say quietly, "Baby, tell me what God feels like. I'm starting to forget.[9]

Reflection

We need to go to children to find out what God feels like. Children have a way of cutting through the guarded responses of an adult world. The child is candid and honest and, as such, seeks out the truth as directly as possible. This is why we get ready for Christmas *one more time.*

We look at the crib scene, in itself a visual artistic prayer, a form for all of us to contemplate. Perhaps that is why some of my friends keep their crib set up all year round.

As we reflect on Christmas, we turn to the crib itself, holding the infant Jesus, helpless, lying there in the straw with Joseph and Mary attentive to his newborn needs. And as the weeks and months drift by, Mary and Joseph will continue to attend to his every need in his utter helplessness.

This infant child contains the mystery of Christmas. We live with a certain lack of understanding till we come to Easter and listen to Mary Magdalen tell us that he—the powerless Rabbi—rose from the dead. He—the victim of political intrigue and religious envy—died naked on a cross at the hands of a Roman execution team. Now he is risen!

The paschal mystery starts with the Christmas mystery. But why should the Messiah, the Christ, come to us as a helpless infant? Why?

We cannot appreciate this mystery unless we become as little children, who see more with their innocent eyes than we do with our developed myopia fixed by our exhaustive experiences of multifaceted reality.

Why believe or hope in Jesus the powerless infant? Perhaps because we start out as little children loving the baby Jesus. Who cannot help but love an infant? A mother enters a room with a baby; all conversation stops, and the infant is treated like a celebrity, a prince, a king. Instinctively we know "kids are special."

Maybe Luke knew this, and Matthew could show how the Gentile world would treat a king that possessed the dignity of infancy. Once a person asked Einstein what value was there in studying astrophysics. He replied by asking: "What value is a baby?"

At Christmas we reflect on the value of the Baby Jesus. Why is any baby valuable? Ahhh. Human hope! Why is the Baby Jesus valuable? Ahhh. Divine hope!—Given to us by God with faith that a helpless infant can change the world.

I wonder about this Christmas mystery, because I want religion to be more efficient than the record shows. I state: "I am grown up. I've been around. What kind of an organization became successful with a venture capital program of twelve less-than-exciting or inspiring apostles?"

Made less by one fallen victim to suicide, the eleven cower sheepishly in an upper room, waiting for something to happen. Here is Jesus, helpless as an infant, dependent on Mary and Joseph, and later powerless as an itinerant preacher, strangely dependent on twelve motley followers. We begin the liturgical year with the preaching of John the Baptist, giving us the hope we need that Jesus will amount to something for our sake.

The story of Sachi brings upon us the full weight of our need to become children so that we can begin to understand the child Jesus. Mature restraint, experienced efficiencies, worldly wisdom? No! None of these will do. We must become as children, simply because children are close to God.

The Anointing at Bethany
or
The Second-to-Last Supper

As we begin this reflection, let us ask that the Spirit of God touch our mind and heart with new understanding of this life as we live it today.

Let us go back two thousand years in time to a small suburb of Jerusalem named Bethany. Let us imagine that we have been invited to a dinner party by one of the leading business and political figures of the community—Simon, a former leper. We sense that this invitation is special, so we walk to the house of Simon with more than the usual stirrings in our celebrating heart.

Simon greets us at the door. He directs a servant to wash our feet and to anoint our face and hands before we proceed to the main dining room. Refreshed from our short journey, we now meet the other guests. We mingle freely in the spacious open area, recognizing a friend here and an acquaintance there. In this respectable group, one figure stands out. He is Jesus, the teacher from Nazareth.

We let the story unfold now as we turn to Mark's Gospel to read his account of the event. Mark says:

Jesus was at Bethany in the house of Simon the leper; he was at dinner when a woman came in with an alabaster jar of very costly ointment, pure nard. She broke the jar and poured the ointment on his head. Some who were there said to one another indignantly, "Why this waste of ointment? Ointment like this could have been sold for over three hundred denarii and the money given to the poor"; and they were angry with her. But Jesus said, "Leave her alone. Why are you upsetting her? What she has done for me is one of the good works. You have the poor with you always, and you can be kind to them whenever you wish, but you will not always have me. She has done what was in her power to do; she has anointed my body beforehand for its burial. I tell you solemnly, wherever throughout all the world the Good News is proclaimed, what she had done will be told also, in remembrance of her."

(Mark 14:3-9)

In the Jewish culture, works of charity were rated as if on a scale. For example, burying the dead was more a work of charity than giving money to the poor. Implicit in this culture is the idea that we assist people throughout life with charitable support. However, as a person approaches death, particularly if he is poor or unjustly translated to that death, the charity toward the dying person becomes more significant, and to anoint a body for burial is one of the greatest acts of love. In recent times we have the example of Mother Teresa. She would pick up a dying person from the streets of Calcutta and take him to her hospice, bathe him and anoint his body, place him between fresh linen, and be present to the person as he approached death.

Here, in the Scriptural story, we have a similar woman, the woman who anoints Jesus. In a few short days Jesus will die, although the woman at Bethany may not have known that fact. Meanwhile we hear the complaint: "Why this waste of ointment? Ointment like this could have been sold for over three hundred denarii and the money given to the poor." In Mother Teresa's mind, as in the mind of this woman at Bethany, a higher charity existed. This was the love that prepared a dying person for death and burial.

Reflection

Let us sharpen our imaginations as we place ourselves at the scene. We see the gathering of guests in the cordial surroundings of Simon the former leper. We hear the warm, friendly conversation. We see the woman (named Mary in John's Gospel) approach Jesus, open up an alabaster jar, and pour out an expensive vial of perfume over his head. Our senses are engaged. We see, we hear; There in our imagination we touch the table and taste the food, but most of all we smell the perfume.

The sense of smell dominates all the other senses. We forget what we see, or hear, or taste, or touch. What we remember most from that scene is what we smell—perfume. Rich perfume, strong expensive essence, as fine as any sold in Paris, London, or Tel Aviv. Perfume worth a year's wages, according to the words of Mark.

Jesus now engages our memory as the perfume touches *his* memory. He says:

> "She has anointed my body beforehand for its burial. I tell you solemnly, wherever throughout all the world the Good News is proclaimed, what she has done will be told also in remembrance of her."

Scientists tell us that, more than any of the other senses, smell locks its impression deep into our memory. So distinct is this bond between smell and memory that, should a particular smell be hidden away for thirty or forty years, all we need is to have this smell return to the olfactory sense and instantly we will visualize the former scene as if it happened only a few seconds ago. The memory of smell is by far the strongest of all our sense memories.

The sense of smell is so unique! We see only when there is sufficient light, taste only when we put things into our mouths, touch only when we make contact with someone or something, hear only sounds that are loud enough, but we smell always and with every breath.[10]

Cover your eyes and you will stop seeing; cover your ears and you will stop hearing. But if you cover your nose and mouth and try to stop smelling, you will die. Etymologically speaking, a breath is not neutral or bland. It is cooked air. We live in a constant simmering. The spirit of life is the breath of life, and the very act of breathing has a smell to it. Smell is the sense that provides a constant signature to life.

Each day we breathe about 23,040 times and move about 438 cubic feet of air. It takes about five seconds to breathe—two seconds to inhale and three seconds to exhale. During that time molecules of odor flood through our breathing system.

Language has difficulty describing smells. However, our memory is quick to record smells. Even so, how does one map out the features of a smell? We use words such as "smoky," "sulfurous," "floral," "fruity," "sweet."

Actually, we are describing smells in terms of other things we know, such as smoke, sulfur, flowers, fruit, and candy.[11] There is a mystery to smells that gives them a kind of magical distance from our original experiences. Smells are special, almost sacred, because they are set apart and we cannot adequately name them.

However, unlike the other senses, smell needs no interpreter. The effect is immediate and undiluted by language, thought, or translation. A smell can be overwhelmingly nostalgic because it triggers powerful images and emotions before we have time to edit them. What we see and hear could fade quickly into the rummage pile of short-term memory. With odors, however, there is no short-term memory.[12] When we give perfume as a gift to someone we care for, we give them liquid memory.

When the woman at Bethany anointed Jesus, Mark identifies the power of the perfume:

—first, to Jesus' memory,

—then, to the memory of all present in the room,

—and finally, to all of us who read the account in Mark's Gospel.

When she poured out the essence of nard on Jesus, she was anointing a king, hidden within the Messianic secret, and only to be revealed later in the memory of the people of God, the Mystical Body of Christ. Over the years, each time the Christian community would gather together, they would call on Christ to be there under the appearances of bread and wine. They would participate in the Eucharist and re-present the Last Supper as a memorial celebration.

Mysteriously this Last Supper becomes linked by perfume to the second-last supper at Bethany. The Messiah of the Last Supper becomes clearly identified as the Messiah in the second-last supper. The word *Messiah* means *anointed one*. According to Mark's version of this story, it was precisely the anointing of Jesus' head that may have caused the evangelist to see this story as a sign of his messiahship, and prefiguring his passion and death about to happen within a few short days. The passion of Jesus becomes the supreme act of the Messiah, and the messiahship of Jesus becomes the Gospel explanation of the passion.[13]

Gerard Manley Hopkins uses this image of oil to remind us of God's grandeur.

He says:

The world is charged with the grandeur of God.
It will flame out like shining from shook foil,
It gathers to a greatness,
Like the ooze of oil crushed.[14]

When the woman poured expensive perfumed nard over the head of Jesus, the grandeur of God mysteriously revealed itself.

Ironically not everything has smell. Only substances volatile enough to spray microscopic particles into the air will touch our olfactory sense. Much of what we encounter in our modern city life—such as stone, glass, and steel—has no inherent smell. Because they do not evaporate particles into air, we do not smell them. By contrast, if you heat incense, it becomes quite volatile and suddenly smells stronger.

Imagine once again sitting at the dinner table with Simon, Jesus, and many others. This unique woman creates an impression that rivets itself deeply into our memory pan. We will not forget the fact that perfumed oil was poured out on the head of Jesus.

Perfume began in Mesopotamia as incense offered to the gods to sweeten the smell of animal flesh burnt as offerings. The Latin etymology tells us how it worked. *Per* meant *through,* and *fumare* meant *to smoke.* Thus, the original sense of *perfumare* was *to burn incense.* Perfumed smoke lifted the things of this earth by air into the realm of the gods.[15] Translated into Jewish ritual, the sacrifices went to God.

Thus, the sacred offering was remembered. The event locked itself into one's memory. The smell would never be forgotten.

We turn to Christ at the Last Supper, his last Passover event, and only a few days after the supper with Simon. He will consecrate bread and wine and ask us to remember. The event of Eucharist, with the smell of perfume still lingering on Jesus' skin, will be a call for all of us to remember that Jesus says: "Do this in memory of me."

Our sensitivity now links the remembrance of the Last Supper to the earlier supper at Bethany:

"I tell you solemnly, wherever throughout the world all the Good News is proclaimed, what she has done will be told also in remembrance of her."

Erase and Repent

Imagine walking down a narrow winding street in twelfth-century Florence. You step hurriedly over sunlit cobblestones on your way to the copyist shop. You are arranging a gift for your brother as he completes the building of his home. You wish to give him a parchment with a poetic message describing your family's joy at this event.

How precious is this parchment. Not only is it expensive, but it is rare. Few people in Florence possess any parchment other than the legal papers kept at the bank or the records office. To possess a personal parchment is rare indeed. And for this occasion no expense is spared.

Metaphor for Life

We compare this parchment to our own human life. In this metaphor we appreciate the full dignity and value of our own personal lives. As the parchment is precious, so too is our life.

Over the years we write on this personal paper. We recount a special time or event. We note a personal contract. We draft an intimate poem. Since we have but one parchment, we begin the habit of erasing the recent work in order to yield this space to a new message. This pragmatic erasure introduces us to a word long obsolete in our daily life—*palimpsest*.

The Oxford English Dictionary tells us that this word of Greek and Latin origins means "a parchment whence writing has been erased." The dictionary continues to list variations of this meaning, such as: "a parchment or other writing-material written upon twice, the original writing having been erased or rubbed out to make place for a second; [or] a manuscript in which a later writing is written over an effaced earlier writing."[16]

The dictionary gives examples from De Quincey and Mrs. Browning, comparing the human brain and the soul respectively to a palimpsest. For me, it seems that it is no stretch to raise the metaphor to an image of my total existence. Initially we each have a rare parchment called life, and in time we need to make erasures. The parchment in its thick-skinned sturdiness accepts these erasures as a matter of course.

Reflection

My Judeo-Christian culture tells me I have but one chance at life here on earth. If I view my life as this sturdy parchment, I allow for much erasing along the way. In effect, my life allows a palimpsestic attitude. If John the Baptist and Jesus of Nazareth (Matthew, chapters 3 and 4) called for repentance—that is, a change of life, habits, and attitude—I can with God's forgiveness erase the past. My birthright allows it.

What a consolation this metaphor creates! My words and deeds become a matter of record, but I can choose to erase the record. My spirit allows me, indeed, at times urges me. I guess I had wished to do everything in life in pencil. But as it happens, I have done many things in ink, not easily erased. Once the recognition of error arises, I look for the apt tools to erase. From rubber erasers to chemicals, I wish to rub out statements of my past. Yet what is so consoling is that my God watches sympathetically and supportively as I erase one error after another from my past.

When we are young, we set our course: pilots of our own ship, navigators of our destiny. Then, surprise! Change. Realistic adjustment for retained hopes. We want our dreams to evolve, not disappear. We want our plans to develop and to reach a satisfying conclusion. Ahhh, not so easy. Outside forces push relentlessly into our life. They change us. They push us in a new direction. Often a more rhapsodic adventure begins. So what do we do? Erase. Write again. New text. New life? Well, not quite. The same parchment, but new words and new ideas.

SPRING

The April Fool—
Jesus Christ

Introduction

(Imagine opera music from the prologue to Leoncavallo's *I Pagliacci*.)

In the midst of this musical introduction, the curtain parts and a man in a clown's costume steps to the footlights. He declares that he is the prologue, and then explains in his aria *"Si Puo, Signore!"* that the story in which he participates is fiction, and the various characters are merely actors. However, he adds that the actors are human beings and are moved by real and powerful emotions. With that introduction the story begins as a play within a play that constantly asks: "What is real?" and "What is imagined?" At times the resemblance to real life is almost too much for Tonio, the lead baritone in the production.

By contrast, we now turn to Christ at the time of his suffering and death. He too may declare that he fulfills his role as the Son of God, but he too is human, and is moved by powerful feelings and emotions. Moreover, we can imagine Christ as a clown who calls us to play out our roles in life as an integral part of his play. All of us are truly human players, and, as human, we experience the full range of emotions that put us in this play called life.

Paul says,

"We are fools for Christ's sake."   (1 Cor 4:10)

43

Reflection

Let us pause and ask ourselves with Paul: Why are we fools and why should we attempt to follow Christ in his role as a clown or fool? In response, we might say that we follow Christ while entertaining many impressions of who he truly is. In so many ways he resembles a clown, a fool, a court jester. His death on the cross is utter foolishness to anyone who does not believe in him. Besides the general theme found in Leoncavallo's *I Pagliacci*, the theme of a clown is found in many places in modern literature.

Perhaps the first person in modern times to give Christ the image of a clown was the artist Georges Rouault. As he boldly brushed this paradoxical image on canvas, he somehow combined the microcosmic reality of a circus and the long tradition of French Christianity. In recent decades the clearest instance of this image of Christ the clown is the film *The Parable* and soon thereafter the musical *Godspell*.

(Pause)

We continue our reflection by placing ourselves in a quiet place, in the quiet presence of our deity. If closing our eyes and leaning more firmly against the back of our chairs assists, by all means do accommodate yourself.

First Image

Let us imagine ourselves in a clown costume, such as found on Tonio in *I Pagliacci*. Jesus is across from us, similarly dressed. He is putting on our make-up. He is telling us that we can be sad clowns or happy clowns. This time he will make us up as sad clowns.

As he applies the make-up, he evokes the sadness of life on our clown face. He reminds us, however, that it is only temporary.

Second Image

Now as we sit in our imaginative clown costume, we change the scene. Let us imagine Christ on Good Friday standing as a clown on Golgotha in a modern clown costume. Let us imagine all the violence of his being nailed to the cross in his clown costume. We hear the pounding of the hammer against the nails, against the flesh, against the wood. What does this image tell me?

We go out on this "Good Friday stage" of Golgotha as clowns, in a crowd mixed with other clowns and non-clowns. We look at the clown Christ hanging on a cross. We will reflect on this scene as part of the crowd of onlookers. We will turn to Matthew's Gospel and read his description of the death of Jesus on the cross. But we begin with Jesus being condemned to death. Matthew says:

> The governor's soldiers took Jesus with them into the Praetorium and collected the whole cohort round him. Then they stripped him and made him wear a scarlet cloak, and having twisted some thorns into a crown they put this on his head and placed a reed in his right hand. To make fun of him they knelt to him saying, "Hail, king of the Jews!" And they spat on him and took the reed and struck him on the head with it. And when they had finished making fun of him, they took off the cloak and dressed him in his own clothes and led him away to crucify him.
>
> On their way out, they came across a man from Cyrene, Simon by name, and enlisted him to carry his cross. When they had reached a place called Golgotha, that is, the place of the skull, they gave him wine to drink mixed with gall, which he tasted but refused to drink. When they had finished crucifying him they shared out his clothing by casting lots, and then sat down and stayed there keeping guard over him.
>
> Above his head was placed the charge against him, it read: "This is Jesus, the King of the Jews." At the same time two robbers were crucified with him, one on the right side and one on the left.

The passersby jeered at him; they shook their heads, and said, "So you would destroy the Temple and rebuild it in three days! Then save yourself! If you are God's son, come down from the cross!" The chief priests with the scribes and elders mocked him in the same way. "He saved others," they said, "he cannot save himself. He is the king of Israel; let him come down from the cross now, and we will believe in him. He puts his trust in God; now let God rescue him if he wants him. For he did say, 'I am the son of God.'" Even the robbers who were crucified with him taunted him in the same way.

From the sixth hour there was darkness over all the land until the ninth hour. And about the ninth hour, Jesus cried out in a loud voice, "Eli, Eli, lama sabachthani?" that is, "My God, my God, why have you deserted me?" When some of those who stood there heard this, they said, "The man is calling on Elijah," and one of them quickly ran to get a sponge which he dipped in vinegar, and, putting it on a reed, gave it to him to drink. "Wait," said the rest of them, "and see if Elijah will come to save him." But Jesus, again crying out in a loud voice, yielded up his spirit.

(Matt 27:27–50)

Strangely enough, this description of Christ on Golgotha was prefigured in the meditative Psalm 22, written about six hundred years before Good Friday. This Psalm is the death prayer of Jesus on the cross. He actually prayed this Psalm as he hung dying.

Let us focus now on Jesus praying quietly on the cross. Let us imagine Jesus the clown reciting this Psalm. Here are some of the key lines he said:

"My God, my God, why have you deserted me?
How far from saving me, the words I groan!

I call all day, my God, but you never answer,
all night long I call and cannot rest.
Yet, Holy One, you
who make your home in the praises of Israel,
in you our fathers put their trust,
they trusted and you rescued them;
they called to you for help and they were saved,
they never trusted you in vain.

"Yet here am I, now more worm than man,
scorn of mankind, jest of the people,
all who see me jeer at me,
they toss their heads and sneer,
'He relied on Yahweh, let Yahweh save him!
If Yahweh is his friend, let Him rescue him!'"   (vv 1–8)

The clown Christ continues in prayer:

"I am like water draining away,
my bones are all disjointed,
my heart is like wax,
melting inside me;
my palate is drier than a potsherd
and my tongue is stuck to my jaw.

"A pack of dogs surround me,
a gang of villains closes me in;
they tie me hand and foot,
and leave me lying in the dust of death.

"I can count every one of my bones,
and there they glare at me, gloating;
they divide my garments among them
and cast lots for my clothes.

"Do not stand aside, Yahweh,
O my strength, come quickly to my help."   (vv 14–19)

With Jesus the clown we beg God to rescue us from the ridicule of the world's outsiders and the press of the fickle crowds on our life...crowds without belief.

Let us ask God to help us realize in faith that, from so much nonsense in the world, there comes sense, and that the plan of God in our life makes sense. As always during this life, we are challenged to find the sense of the cross with a clown hanging on it.

Paul often reflected on the foolishness of the cross. Let us turn to a passage of Paul in his letter to the Romans that draws us to the hope of Easter Sunday:

> After saying this, what can we add? With God on our side who can be against us? Since God did not spare his own Son, but gave him up to benefit us all, we may be certain, after such a gift, that he will not refuse anything he can give. Could anyone accuse those that God has chosen? When God acquits, could anyone condemn? Could Christ Jesus? No! He not only died for us—he rose from the dead, and there at God's right hand he stands and pleads for us.
>
> Nothing therefore can come between us and the love of Christ, even if we are troubled or worried, or being persecuted, or lacking food or clothes, or being threatened or even attacked.
>
> For I am certain of this: neither death nor life, nor angel, or prince, nothing that exists, nothing still to come, not any power, or height or depth, nor any created thing, can ever come between us and the love of God made visible in Christ Jesus our Lord.
>
> (Rom 8:31–39)

I ask that you place your personal conclusion to these Scriptures, keeping in mind the theme of Paul:

"We are fools for Christ's sake."

We also hold in memory Paul's other statement:

"The foolishness of God is wiser than men, and God's weakness is stronger than human strength."

(1 Cor 1:25)

Service and Leadership

In Luke's Gospel we read:

> A dispute also arose among them as to which one of them was to be regarded as the greatest. But he said to them, "The kings of the Gentiles lord it over them; and those in authority over them are called benefactors. But not so with you; rather the greatest among you must become like the youngest, and the leader like one who serves. For who is greater, the one who is at the table or the one who serves? Is it not the one at the table? But I am among you as one who serves."
>
> (Luke 22:24–27)

The last line of the passage is traced in bold letters around the copula sheltering the main altar of the Cathedral of St. James in Seattle. "I am among you as one who serves."

Reflection

I imagine the enduring patience of Jesus at the time of his Last Supper with his apostles. At this most solemn event the apostles are arguing over rank and power. They know clearly they will be leaders. But they fail to recognize that service is to characterize their leadership.

When we turn to John's Gospel and read about the Last Supper, we find another dramatic reference to service. Instead of Jesus giving a "pep talk" to the future leaders of the Christian community, he begins the meal by placing a towel around his waist and then proceeds to wash the feet of each of his apostles. Peter was shocked. This gesture, it appears, was meant to shock.

At the Last Supper we see Jesus the teacher carrying out a lesson for his apostles, the students. Jesus shows them that all learning is a shared experience between teacher and students. Both share the same reality, namely, our common world in time and space. Both teacher (Jesus) and students (the apostles) are vulnerable to the power of our natural environment. If we take the place of the apostles, we recognize that we too are thrown into a world not of our own making. We feel powerless, destined to suffer and die. In the final analysis we are totally alone and unable to rescue others from these common realities. Our weakness is our unity, our solidarity. Our service is a recognition of a need to be liberated from the slavery of sin and pettiness and all the various accidents of nature around us. Jesus teaches us as he carries on a real conversation about life. He speaks in a manner both humble and bold. He has shown his accomplishments by showing his desire to serve others and not lord it over the apostles.

When I was a student in high school in the early '50s, I was part of a rather simple life. One person of service stands out in my memory. His name was Herb Wolf. He was the secretary. In practice he ran the school. Oh, St. Francis had a principal, a faculty, and staff members. But Herb Wolf was at the center of our school life as the secretary, registrar, class scheduler, substitute parent, consoler, and confidant for each of us. He was a leader and he was the servant of us all.

Herb suffered paralysis from polio. He needed special crutches to move around and could not go any distance without a wheelchair. Somehow we never noticed his disabilities. His warm smile and his supportive voice seemed to fill out our image of who he was.

I believe most schools and most institutions have people like Herb Wolf. My classmates and I could barely go a day without visiting him and trying to get a reaction of some sort from him to meet our teenage needs. Herb was the ideal leader and the effective servant. He was there. He was aware. He cared.

When World War II brought us the controlling diabolical leadership of Hitler and Mussolini, I learned a new meaning of the word "leader." Hitler was called *Der Führer,* and Mussolini, *Il Duce.* Both words literally meant "leader." Yet after the war Germany and Italy excised those words from their public vocabulary. After 1945 those words never again appeared in the German or Italian press.

Service and leadership have built-in dangers. Too dedicated a service will bring fatigue. Too controlling a leadership will take away shared responsibility within the community. If we learn to collaborate as Christian members of a faith community, we discover that we can bring our energies to the common cause without yielding to the built-in dangers of service and leadership.

The Chinese invented the idea of civil service. The British fine-tuned the idea and developed a system of ministries for each department of government. The primitive Christian community introduced the office of deacon as service to the poor. Curiously the words "minister," "servant," and "deacon" hold the same meaning in Latin, English, and Greek respectively.

We return to the reading in St. Luke's Gospel. We stop to reflect on our place in the community. We think of our own individual gifts that we bring to the community. We ask once again as we reread this text: "How do I serve; how do I lead?"

A dispute also arose among them as to which one of them was to be regarded as the greatest. But he said to them, "The kings of the Gentiles lord it over them; and those in authority over them are called benefactors. But not so with you; rather the greatest among you must become like the youngest, and the leader like one who serves. For who is greater, the one who is at the table or the one who serves? Is it not the one at the table? But I am among you as one who serves."

(Luke 22:24–27)

The Eucharist

Introduction

The highest expression of our personal and communal faith is the eucharistic celebration. We take time now to reflect upon the position of the Eucharist in our spiritual life.

We will be viewing the Eucharist as if in three different settings or three different tables.

First, we will talk about and pray about the Last Supper, the Passover celebration, the night before Jesus died.

Second, we will talk about a table in a restaurant, with a young couple taking supper together.

Third, we will speak of the banquet table of the eucharistic Jesus who invites us to share in our present day worship, at our local church or congregation.

Let's begin by placing ourselves in a comfortable position in this setting. Let us call on God to be with us, to direct our thoughts and prayers today. Let us calmly take a few breaths, listening to our breathing, hoping that we all relax and open our hearts to the Spirit.

Reflection

The First Table

We begin by talking about the first table, the table of the Last Supper. We read in Matthew, chapter 26:

Now on the first day of Unleavened Bread the disciples came to Jesus to say, "Where do you want us to make the preparations for you to eat the Passover?" "Go to so-and-so in the city," he replied, "and say to him, "The Master says: My time is near. It is at your house that I am keeping Passover with my disciples." The disciples did what Jesus told them and prepared the Passover. (vv 17–19)

After a few verses Matthew continues:

Now as they were eating, Jesus took some bread, and when he had said the blessing he broke it and gave it to the disciples. "Take it and eat"; he said, "this is my body." Then he took a cup, and when he had returned thanks he gave it to them. "Drink all of you from this," he said, "for this is my blood, the blood of the covenant, which is to be poured out for many for the forgiveness of sins. From now on, I tell you, I shall not drink wine until the day I drink the new wine with you in the kingdom of my Father." (vv 26–29)

Prayerfully I now ask some questions:

How do I sense Christ in the Eucharist?

I taste the bread and the wine, but what assimilation takes place?

Does Christ become a part of me? Do I become a part of Christ?

I have gone to Holy Communion many, many times. But where is this Christ in my life? I look around. Did not my community receive Christ? Can I not find Christ in them? Especially when he is absent or seemingly absent from my own personal life?

The Second Table

Now let us pray over our second scene, a small table in a restaurant with a young couple seated one across from the other, their eyes fixed on each other, their one hand joined across the table in a romantic clasp.

Their very gaze speaks a story of love and joy that young couples show in such a restaurant setting. When I look at them I ask: What do I see?

Not simply two people eating a meal, but a couple showing a special relationship of love. This element catches us as we meditate on the riches of the Eucharist. In the Eucharist there is not simply God in Christ coming under the appearances of bread and wine, or we receiving the Eucharist. But the Eucharist expresses our relationship: God and me—united in love by the eucharistic communion.

The relationship has a life of its own—strong enough to move persons beyond their individuality to respond to God's will by going out into the world nourished with the *food of relationship*. There is a special strength inherent in the Eucharist.

The Third Table

Now let us imagine the third table—the place where we usually receive the Eucharist, such as our home church, whether on a Sunday or a weekday. When we approach the Eucharist, we come to a foreshadowing of our heavenly banquet and a re-presentation of the Last Supper.

Our eyes see bread and wine, but our minds and hearts look behind it and see the community calling Christ to be present under the appearances of bread and wine, and our spirit, our whole being, mind and heart, expressing faith with that community.

We now reflect that we come to the Eucharist to be nourished. We want more than ordinary bread; we want the bread that nourishes us forever. But this faith calls for alert participation.

Mother Teresa says: "There is hunger for ordinary bread and there is hunger for love, for kindness, for thoughtfulness; and this is the great poverty that makes people suffer so much."

As we approach the eucharistic table at our own church, we are reminded that Christ invites all people to the banquet—rich and poor alike. No one is left out, especially the poor, especially sinners. John the Baptist preached to sinners; local rabbis exorcised evil spirits from them; and Jesus ate with them.

Jesus went out of his way to mix socially with beggars, tax collectors, outcasts, and prostitutes. That expression of love shocked the society that separated neatly all classes of people. We pray now that we learn how to take this charity away from the banquet into our daily life and restrict no one from our daily service.

We repeat the prayer of a hill tribe in Northern Bengal:

If I ask him for a gift, he will give it to me, and then I shall have to go away. But I do not want to go away. Give me no gift, give me yourself. I want to be with you, my beloved.[17]

Ultimately, that is what the apostles wished at the Last Supper, and the young couple in the restaurant, and we at our local church.

Give me no gift, give me yourself.

Good and Evil

From Persia to Palestine along the familiar caravan trails of the Fertile Crescent, each cultural grouping looked for a reasonable explanation of good and evil. As opposites, good and evil fought for air-time in a close knit family. As siblings, both struggled for identity within the developing family of religions of the world. Jewish monotheism declared that the God of good was clearly in charge, but evil had his day. In Greek polytheism both good and evil contended as gods.

Today more than in the past, life is accepted as a seamless whole. We accept the idea of a good God, but we witness the harsh realities of evil in our midst. Our ethicists tell us the issue is free will, exercised deliberately in various cultures with a panoply of motivations. Eventually we learn to live with both good and evil competing endlessly for our human attention.

Within this experience we cannot easily assess our free choices. We constantly ask if this choice, this moment, or that choice, the next moment, is basically good or evil. If our life is more than individual atomic events, we look for a pattern that paints a consistent picture. We use phrases like "fundamental option" to describe the consistent good we yearn for.

Once our faith in God feels strong, we begin to estimate how we relate to this mysterious friend who cares about us more than we care about ourselves. Even the mystics like Teresa of Avila wondered why things happened to her the way they did, if God truly loved her.

Our human condition pulls us back to reality: "God's ways are not our ways" (paraphrasing Isaiah, chapter 55). Whatever happens to us is part of the mystery of life, the sweet mystery of life—as the song goes.

In the Taoist mind the good and evil we experience are not clear ideas. Moreover, they are not necessarily opposite ideas. One easily blends with the other. Huston Smith tells the Taoist story of a farmer who was trying to figure out whether events in his life were a blessing or a punishment. As the story goes, the farmer had a horse that ran away. His neighbor shared his sadness with the farmer only to hear from the farmer's lips: "Who knows what is good or bad?" The next day the horse returned bringing with him a small herd of wild horses he befriended. The neighbor reappeared with congratulations for the windfall. The farmer responded once again: "Who knows what is good or bad?" The next day the farmer's son tried to mount one of the wild horses and fell, breaking his leg. The neighbor once again shared his sadness with the farmer. Again the farmer responded: "Who knows what is good or bad?" The following day soldiers came to the farmer's home seeking out new conscripts for the army. The son was exempted because of his injury.[18]

Reflection

This Taoist story is also Zen-like, mixing easily with Buddhist thought. Like Ecclesiastes in the Hebrew Scriptures, life and death, apparent good and apparent evil, blend as complementary cycles. What happens to us is a part of the whole. The challenge for us is to be able to see the whole when only a part is easily visible. Alfred Tennyson held a similar view in his poem "Oh Yet We Trust":

Oh yet we trust that somehow good
    Will be the final goal of ill,
    To pangs of nature, sins of will,
Defects of doubt, and taints of blood;

That nothing walks with aimless feet;
    That not one life shall be destroyed,
    Or cast as rubbish to the void,
When God hath made the pile complete;

That not a worm is cloven in vain;
    That not a moth with vain desire
    Is shriveled in a fruitless fire,
Or but subserves another's gain.

Behold, we know not anything;
    We can but trust that good shall fall
    At last—far off—at last, to all
And every winter change to spring.

So runs my dream; but what am I?
    An infant crying in the night:
    An infant crying for the light:
And with no language but a cry.[19]

In our relationship with God we become both humble and honest. Like infants we come to admit that we do not know why various things happen to us. However, we are open to learn as time unfolds. Our theological awareness develops with our experience. And the more we reflect, the more the events of our lives begin to become ever so slightly more understandable.

SUMMER

Forgiveness

The ballads of our culture are songs of love. Hebrew and Christian writings consider love the highest of virtues. As if by nature all of us strive to love and be loved in return. Yet a basic dimension of love is the difficult challenge of forgiveness. Perhaps that may be the reason why so much literature talks about this requirement and the opposite nefarious force called revenge. Time has taught us the sadness of seeking revenge.

In Buddhist literature we find the Kshanti Paramita,[20] or the capacity to receive, carry, and transform the pain imposed upon us. Imagine you have finished a long walk. You stop at a campsite and pour a cup of fresh water from a spigot. The water is pure, fresh, and cold, coming directly from a mountain stream. You anticipate the refreshment as you begin to draw the cup to your lips. For a prank, a friend next to you pours a tablespoon of salt into your cup. Oh! Disgusting! I cannot drink this water. It is ruined by the salt.

You yearn to have clean water, but you need to go away from the prankster. You walk to a serene spring-fed mountain lake sitting as a round blue gem in the middle of uneven banks of Douglas fir. You go to the shore and put your cup into this clear crystal lake. Ah! The prankster has not disappeared. He is there with his salt. He throws a tablespoon of salt into the lake only seconds before you draw out a cup of fresh water. Ah! No problem! Why? The tablespoon of salt is lost among the thousands of gallons of pure fresh water. His prank cannot affect you.

Reflection

We use this comparison for our meditation today. The prankster is the person in our life who says or does something that hurts us and makes us angry. How do we cope?

We must place ourselves in the position of the person seeking refreshing water. If we only have a cup of water, the salt of the prankster will irritate us and cause us to stop the process of moving toward a refreshing drink. What do we do? We expand that limited cup and make it a mountain lake. We take our personality and expand our source of water from that of a cup to that of a lake. The lake is so large that it cannot suffer the small difference of a tablespoon of salt.

In our prayer we expand our capacity to receive and transform pain. If my heart is small, one unjust word or act will make me suffer. If I expand my heart, allowing for understanding and compassion, the word or deed no longer will cause pain. I will be able to receive the hurt and mix it into the vast lake that embraces and transforms any small hurt that comes to it. What matters here is my capacity. What matters, furthermore, is my ability to accept the grace of God to expand my capacity.

Let us sit silently with these images. We look deeply into our hearts. Let us imagine that we can expand our heart to include all the little negative comments and idle gossip that cause pain. Someone else is out there with salt to pour into the expanse of our lives. If we have abundant capacity, we can embrace this hurt and mix it into the clear crystal serenity of our lives.

If we are at peace with God and with our community, one hurtful comment will not diminish the capacity to seek normal routine refreshment from the lake of our personality.

Sometimes you and I feel that our capacity is small and, under some circumstances, growing smaller by degrees. We must stop and, in our prayer, expand the clear waters of our personality to larger and larger capacity.

Let's take a minute to dwell on the image of expanding our lake. We call on God to stretch our heart and mind to a fuller awareness of life. Let us imagine this lake high in the mountain forest expanding slowly and silently, filling out a larger and larger space in this mountain forest.

We speak to God humbly:

"Expand my capacity, so that I can accept the daily table-spoons of pain poured into my life. Help me, God, to nourish and expand this capacity of love and forgiveness for any hurt that meets me. Help me, God, to take up this portion, this salty portion of pain, and transform it into a broad expanse of love and understanding.

"Be with me, God, and let my lake of compassion grow! May all hurt that meets me meet a cool serene lake of love that accepts and transforms this hurt into a greater portion of love and understanding. O God, let my lake of love grow!"

God the Communicator

The idea of God is so expansive that we wonder how God can possibly communicate with us poor mortals. What follows is a modern parable found in the book *St. George and the Dragon*, by Edward Hays.

Reflection

It was the Review Board weekend in heaven, and God had once again convened his committee of angels to review the activities of creation. God was at the head of a long conference table, and a committee of angels and archangels was seated around it. Each had a manila folder containing reports on the various aspects of creation. These Review Board meetings were times of great importance and excitement, for it was at these meetings that God presented new ideas for the evaluation of the angelic committee.

"Before we go over our reports," God said with a smile, "I would like to ask your opinions on an idea that came to me the other night." Several angels nodded their heads, while others moved restlessly in their chairs. They were uneasy whenever God began this way because it required a diplomat's skill to discuss an idea that wasn't practical. Naturally, some angels agreed with every idea that God presented, even with the ones that were, to put it plainly, more than impractical, they were dumb—but, mind you, divinely dumb!

God wore a big smile, which only made the more conservative angels very nervous. They had learned over the millennia that the larger the smile, the more out-landish was the idea.

"I feel," said God, "that it's time for me to speak more directly to my children on earth. Until now I have spoken to them by means of a flood, fire, rainbows and, of course, a quiet whisper in the heart of certain chosen ones. But I feel that they need to hear more directly from me—to let them know the feelings of my heart, my dreams and my ideas on how to correct the problems they always seem to be getting themselves into. So...," and here God paused and smiled again, "I think I should come to earth in human form, as one of them!"

Gasps and moans rose from around the conference table. The more timid angels quickly opened their manila folders and began nervously shuffling through their reports. God chuckled inwardly. He hadn't seen such a response from the Celestial Committee since he had sprung his idea of creating Adam on them.

One of the angels finally spoke. "Lord God, your idea certainly has merit. But don't we already have in place an excellent system for any messages you might want to send to earth? You have us, your angelic messengers who are willing to fly anywhere at any hour. Why do we need a new form of communication?"

"Too limited and too exclusive," responded God. "And it usually frightens the mortals when one of you angels suddenly materializes in front of them. No, we need a better means of reaching as many of them as possible."

"Lord God," suggested another angel on the committee, "your idea is intriguing. But I fear that it is not time yet for you to come to earth as one of them. My opinion, from all the reports I've seen, is that it will take at least three thousand more years before any such idea should be tried, and even then..." But the angel was interrupted by a chorus of voices.

"Lord God," chimed in an earnest archangel, "to come in human form would be beneath your dignity. And if you come, Lord, which race would you choose? Think of the complications of even the choice of skin color! Imagine how the others would feel if you single out one race: the resentment and envy, not to mention the charge of a 'special friendship.'"

"And, Lord God," spoke another voice, a deep bass voice that drowned out all the others, "which sex would you choose? Consider well such folly and how it will cause untold theological problems. Think of the discrimination; one sex will deeply resent the implication that you so favor the other."

At this point the committee members began to argue vigorously with one another, and one whispered, "Well, Yahweh's done it again—we might as well junk the agenda of this meeting!"

"Friends, friends...quiet, please, quiet!" said God. "I hear your many objections and concerns. Indeed the problems you raise are valid. It's just that I'm so impatient, so eager to see my creation become what I dream it can. Perhaps I *am* in too great a hurry to resolve the first-stage problems of my wonderful experiment of Adam and Eve. You are probably correct in thinking it may take another three or four thousand years before they will be ready. And if I hear you correctly, some of you feel that the problems of which sex, race, or nationality to choose may make it an eternal impossible dream."

The silence that followed was like that of many a meeting—a blend of disappointment and frustration for some, a sense of victory for others, and questions still hanging in the air. The static stillness around the conference table was broken by the voice of one angel. "My Lord God, why not come to earth in the form of writing? Your children, the Sumerians, have perfected the earlier experiments of expressing messages and ideas by making marks, by the use of symbolic figures. And the Egyptians and Chinese are making some rather remarkable breakthroughs in its technology. You could come to earth in the form of hieroglyphics—as letters of the alphabet!"

"Marvelous idea," shouted God, "marvelous...yes, that's it! I will come as letters of the alphabet. I shall come as word!"

"But Lord God," said the bass-voiced angel, "which alphabet will you be? Egyptian, Chinese, Hittite, Hebrew, or Greek? Isn't that the same problem as having to choose between the races? No, Lord God, you cannot be partial! You cannot discriminate and still be God! At least not if you are to be who you are—the God of all of them! No, you must stay with the old ways and continue to speak to them in flood, fire, and the rainbow. These are universal containers for your messages. We have no need for any novel forms. The old will continue to serve us well." As the angel finished, a short burst of applause expressed the agreement of many.

Under the conference table, unseen by the members of the Review Board, God's foot tapped in anger and impatience. If the angels had seen the divine toe tap-tap-tapping, they easily would have decoded its message: "Why are they so afraid of anything new and untried? They think that Adam was a big mistake; but I think a bigger one was the creation of the committees!"

In the silence that followed, all faces were turned toward the head of the table where God sat with closed eyes, lost in deep thought. Slowly God opened one eye, then the other—and looked directly at the angel who had proposed that God come to earth as letters in the alphabet and who, at this point, was nervously chewing at the end of a yellow pencil. "You say that this invention of writing has great potential?" asked God. "Can we rightly foresee that they will continue to improve on their earlier experiments and that some day everyone will be able to read? And that by means of written words they will be able to understand the most abstract of ideas?"

"Yes, Lord God," replied the angel. "With written words you could prepare them for your coming in human form. You could speak without causing the fear of your thunderbolt messages and more clearly than using rainbows, which can mean almost anything. But my distinguished angelic colleague, I fear, is correct. You would have to choose one of many alphabets. No, I withdraw my suggestion; it is of no value."

"Far from it, my clever friend," responded God, who once again was wearing a wide, expansive grin. "Far from it! Because I have decided—after careful consideration of your suggestions and objections—I have decided to come into the world as ink!"

"INK?" gasped the angels.

"Yes, ink!" replied God. "Then I can reside in the letters of *all* alphabets. I shall come to earth in the alphabets of the Egyptians and the Hebrews, in Chinese and Sanskrit, in Greek and Latin, in Russian and...well, the possibilities are unlimited...unlimited!"

And here our parable ends, except for this brief postscript. God did indeed come into the world as ink. And the people of earth recognized the Divine Presence in the Hebrew letters of the *Torah*, in the Sanskrit of the Vedic books of India, and in the Chinese characters of the *Tao Te Ching*. With reverence they bowed before the Arabic letters of the *Koran* and illuminated the Greek and Latin of the Gospels with gold leaf. Just as God said at that Review Board meeting, "The possibilities are unlimited."[21]

Authentic Personhood

We spend a lifetime trying to figure out who we are. When we think we have the answer, we discover that we still are growing, changing, and redefining the characteristics of our personality. We are all human, but we like to think that our ideals and our work can raise us above the simple limits of living.

Robert Fulghum tells a story of a peacemaker who will become familiar to us as the story unfolds.

Reflection

There is a person who has profoundly disturbed my peace of mind for a long time. She doesn't even know me, but she continually goes around minding my business. We have very little in common. She is an old woman, an Albanian who grew up in Yugoslavia; she is a Roman Catholic nun who lives in poverty in India. I disagree with her on fundamental issues of population control, the place of women in the world and in the church, and I am turned off by her naive statements about "what God wants." She stands at the center of great contradictory notions and strong forces that shape human destiny. She drives me crazy. I get upset every time I hear her name or read her words or see her face. I don't even want to talk about her.

In the studio where I work, there is a wash basin. Above the wash basin is a mirror. I stop at this place several times each day to tidy up and look at myself in the mirror. Alongside the mirror is a photograph of the troublesome woman. Each time I look in the mirror at myself, I also look at her face. In it I have seen more than I can tell; and from what I see, I understand more than I can say.

The photograph was taken in Oslo, Norway, on the tenth of December, in 1980. This is what happened there:

A small, stooped woman in a faded blue sari and worn sandals received an award. From the hand of a king. An award funded from the will of the inventor of dynamite. In a great glittering hall of velvet and gold and crystal. Surrounded by the noble and famous in formal black and in elegant gowns. The rich, the powerful, the brilliant, the talented of the world in attendance. And there at the center of it all—a little old lady in sari and sandals. Mother Teresa, of India. Servant of the poor and sick and dying. To her, the Nobel Peace Prize.

No shah or president or king or general or scientist or pope; no banker or merchant or cartel or oil company or ayatollah holds the key to as much power as she has. None is as rich. For hers is the invincible weapon against the evils of this earth: the caring heart. And hers are the everlasting riches of this life: the wealth of the compassionate spirit.

To cut through the smog of helpless cynicism, to take only the tool of uncompromising love; to make manifest the capacity for healing humanity's wounds; to make the story of the Good Samaritan a living reality; and to live so true a life as to shine out from the back streets of Calcutta takes courage and faith we cannot admit in ourselves and cannot be without.

I do not speak her language. Yet the eloquence of her life speaks to me. And I am chastised and blessed at the same time. I do not believe one person can do much in this world. Yet there she stood, in Oslo, affecting the world around. I do not believe in her version of God. But the power of her faith shames me. And I believe in Mother Teresa.

73

December in Oslo. The message for the world at Christmastide is one of peace. Not the peace of a child asleep in the manger of long ago. Nor the peace of a full dinner and a nap by the fire on December 25. But a tough, vibrant, vital peace that comes from the extraordinary gesture one simple woman in a faded sari and worn sandals makes this night. A peace of mind that comes from a piece of work.

Some years later, at a grand conference of quantum physicists and religious mystics at the Oberoi Towers Hotel in Bombay, I saw that face again. Standing by the door at the rear of the hall, I sensed a presence beside me. And there she was. Alone. Come to speak to the conference as its guest. She looked at me and smiled. I see her face still.

She strode to the rostrum and changed the agenda of the conference from intellectual inquiry to moral activism. She said, in a firm voice to the awed assembly: "We can do no great things; only small things with great love."

The contradictions of her life and faith are nothing compared to my own. And while I wrestle with frustration about the impotence of the individual, she goes right on changing the world. While I wish for more power and resources, she uses her power and resources to do what she can do at the moment.

She upsets me, disturbs me, shames me. *What does she have that I do not?*

If ever there is truly peace on earth, goodwill to men, it will be because of women like Mother Teresa. Peace is not something you *wish* for; it's something you *make,* something you *do,* something you *are,* and something you *give away!*[22]

Faith, Tradition, and Love

Often one topic leads naturally to thoughts of an allied topic. This becomes true when we discuss faith. Thinking and reflecting on one's personal faith lead readily to thoughts about our tradition. Then we can turn our mind to thoughts about the expression of our faith and tradition in love.

We will examine three short stories or tales that point up the richness of the three topics: faith, tradition, and love.

Reflection

The first story tells of a bishop making a visitation to some remote islands in the Pacific.

Story of Faith

When the bishop's ship stopped at a remote island for a day, he determined to use the time as profitably as possible. He strolled along the seashore and came across three fishermen mending their nets. In pidgin English they explained to him that centuries before they had been Christianized by missionaries. "We Christians!" they said, proudly pointing to one another. The bishop was impressed. Did they know the Lord's Prayer? They had never heard of it. The bishop was shocked.

"What do you say, then, when you pray?"

"We lift eyes to heaven. We pray, 'We are three, you are three, have mercy on us.'"

The bishop was appalled at the primitive, the downright heretical nature of their prayer. So he spent the whole day teaching them the Lord's Prayer. The fishermen were poor learners, but they gave it all they had and before the bishop sailed away the next day he had the satisfaction of hearing them go through the whole formula without a fault.

Months later, the bishop's ship happened to pass by those islands again, and the bishop, as he paced the deck saying his evening prayers, recalled with pleasure the three men on that distant island who were now able to pray, thanks to his patient efforts. While he was lost in that thought, he happened to look up and noticed a spot of light in the east. The light kept approaching the ship, and as the bishop gazed in wonder, he saw three figures walking on the water. The captain stopped the ship, and everyone leaned over the rails to see this sight.

When they were within speaking distance, the bishop recognized his three friends, the fishermen. "Bishop!" they exclaimed. "We hear your boat go past island and come hurry hurry meet you."

"What is it you want?" asked the awe-stricken bishop.

"Bishop," they said, "we so, so sorry. We forget lovely prayer. We say, 'Our Father in heaven, holy be your name, your kingdom come...' then we forget. Please tell us prayer again."

The bishop felt humbled. "Go back to your homes, my friend," he said, "and each time you pray say, 'We are three, you are three, have mercy on us!'"[23]

Stories are such effective teachers! When we think of tradition, we deal immediately with an abstract word. Perhaps the following story will move us from the abstraction to a concrete understanding of how we live out our faith.

Tradition

When the founder of Hasidic Judaism, the great Rabbi Israel Shem Tov, saw misfortune threatening the Jews, it was his custom to go into a certain part of the forest to meditate. There he would light a fire, say a special prayer, and the miracle would be accomplished and the misfortune averted.

Later, when his disciple, the celebrated Maggid of Mezritch, had occasion, for the same reason, to intercede with heaven, he would go to the same place in the forest and say: "Master of the Universe, listen! I do not know how to light the fire, but I am still able to say the prayer," and again the miracle would be accomplished.

Still later, Rabbi Moshe-leib of Sasov, in order to save his people once more, would go into the forest and say, "I do not know how to light the fire. I do not know the prayer, but I know the place and this must be sufficient." It was sufficient, and the miracle was accomplished.

Then it fell to Rabbi Israel of Rizhin to overcome misfortune. Sitting in his armchair, his head in his hands, he spoke to God: "I am unable to light the fire, and I do not know the prayer, and I cannot even find the place in the forest. All I can do is to tell the story, and this must be sufficient."

And it was sufficient.

For God made man because he loves stories.[24]

Love

Religion is not a mere intellectual exercise of faith. Realistically, faith must be expressed in our day-to-day life. For Christians there is the constancy of the Gospels urging us to recognize the place of charity or love in our daily lives. What follows is a simple story of brotherly love:

Time before time, when the world was young, two brothers shared a field and a mill. Each night they divided evenly the grain they had ground together during the day. Now as it happened, one of the brothers lived alone; the other had a wife and a large family. One day, the single brother thought to himself: "It isn't really fair that we divide the grain evenly. I have only myself to care for, but my brother has children to feed." So each night he secretly took some of his grain to his brother's granary to see that he was never without.

But the married brother said to himself one day, "It isn't really fair that we divide the grain evenly, because I have children to provide for me in my old age, but my brother has no one. What will he do when he is old?" So every night he secretly took some of his grain to his brother's granary. As a result, both of them always found their supply of grain mysteriously replenished each morning.

Then one night the brothers met each other halfway between their two houses, suddenly realized what had been happening, and embraced each other in love. The story is that God witnessed their meeting and proclaimed, "This is a holy place—a place of love—and here it is that my temple shall be built." And so it was. The holy place, where God is made known, is the place where human beings discover each other in love.[25]

Notes

1. All references to Sacred Scripture are taken from *The Jerusalem Bible* (London: Darton, Longman, and Todd, 1966).

2. Paul Tillich, *The Courage to Be* (London: Collins Clear-Type Press, 1952).

3. Marianne Moore, *The Complete Poems of Marianne Moore* (New York: The Macmillan Publishing Co. Inc., Penguin Books, 1967), 95ff.

4. Taken from the liturgy of Ash Wednesday.

5. Ernest Dawson, "Vitae Summa Brevis Spem Nos Vetat Incohare Longam," in *A Treasury of Great Poems*, Vol. II, ed. Louis Untermeyer (New York: Simon and Schuster, 1955), 1049.

6. Reinhold Niebuhr, *The Irony of American History* (New York: Scribner, 1952), 73.

7. Walt Whitman, "Leaves of Grass," in *A Treasury of Great Poems*, 896.

8. The quotations in this reflection come from a variety of quotation collections, such as *The Treasure Chest*, ed. Charles L. Wallis (San Francisco: Harper Collins Publishers, 1995); *The Penguin Dictionary of Quotations*, eds. J. M. and M. S. Cohen (Middlesex, England: Penguin Books, 1960); *5000 Quotations for all Occasions*, ed. Lewis C. Henry (Philadelphia: The Blakiston Co., 1945). However, most of the references come from *The New Dictionary of Thoughts*, ed. Tryon Edwards (New York: Standard Book Co., 1959), 246–47.

9. Dan Millman, "Sachi," in *Chicken Soup for the Soul*, eds. Jack Canfield and Mark Victor Hansen (Deerfield Beach, FL: Health Communications Inc., 1993), 290.

10. Diane Ackerman, *A Natural History of the Senses* (New York: Vintage Books, 1990), 6–63.

11. Ibid., 11. All smells fall into a few basic categories: minty (peppermint), floral (roses), ethereal (pears), musky (musk), resinous (cam-

phor), foul (rotten eggs), acrid (vinegar). Taste, by contrast, has four fla-
vors: sweet, sour, salt, and bitter.

12. Ibid.

13. This idea is expressed more fully in D. E. Nieham, *St. Mark*
(Middlesex, England: Penguin Books, 1963), 372–73; also Vincent Taylor,
The Gospel According to St. Mark (London: Macmillan & Co. Ltd., 1966).

14. Gerard Manley Hopkins, "God's Grandeur," in *A Treasury of
Great Poems*, 978.

15. Ackerman, 56.

16. James A. H. Murray et al. (ed.), *The Oxford English Dictionary*
(Oxford: Clarendon Press, 1961), vii, 393.

17. Ascribed to the oral tradition of a hill tribe in Northern Bengal.
Quoted in *The Oxford Book of Prayer*, George Appleton, ed. (Oxford:
Oxford University Press, 1988), 297.

18. Huston Smith, *The World's Religions* (New York: Harper Collins
Publishers, 1991), 215–16.

19. Taken from *Prayers for the Classroom*, ed. Philip Verhalen
(Collegeville, MN: Liturgical Press, 1998), 121.

20. Trich Nhat Hanh, *The Heart of Buddha's Teaching* (New York:
Broadway Books, 1998), 193–205.

21. Edward Hays, *St. George and the Dragon* (Leavenworth, KS:
Forest of Peace Publishing Inc., 1986), 44–49.

22. Robert Fulghum, *All I Really Need to Know I Learned in
Kindergarten* (New York: Ivy Books by Ballantine Books, 1988), 189–92.

23. This is a shortened version of a story by Anthony de Mello, SJ,
from his collection *The Song of the Bird* (Anand, India: Gujaret Sahitya
Prakash, 1982), 88–89.

24. A variation of this story is found in several works, one of which
is Elie Wiesel, *The Gates of the Forest* (New York: Holt, Rinehart, and
Winston, 1967), 73.

25. Ernest Kurtz and Katherine Ketcham, *The Spirituality of Imper-
fection* (New York: Bantam Books, 1994), 9–10.

A Brief Book List
on Prayer

Basic Reading

Cassidy, Sheila. *Prayer for Pilgrims*. New York: Crossroad Publishing Co., 1980. Short essays on the role of prayer in our normal lives. A solid response to the problems of praying.

Forsyth, P. T. *The Soul of Prayer*. Vancouver, B.C.: Regent College Publishers, 1997. First published in 1915, the work creates awareness of our regard for different kinds of prayer depending on our needs.

Foster, Richard J. *Prayer*. San Francisco: Harper Collins Publishers, 1992. A variety of types of prayer treated as separate topics and sensitive to changing needs. Engaging!

Huggett, Joyce. *Learning the Language of Prayer*. New York: Crossroad Publishing Co. 1994. This author sets a structure for developing one's prayer life. For many of us, more practical than other texts.

Van Zeller, Dom Hubert. *Approach to Prayer*. New York: Sheed and Ward, 1958. A brief, clear, and concise exposition of all the elements needed to intensify our prayer life.

Further Reading about Prayer

Casey, Michael. *Toward God*. Liguouri, MO: Triumph Books, 1996. Compelling essays on the appreciation of prayer in our lives.

Castro, Emilio. *When We Pray Together*. Geneva, Switzerland: W.C.C. Publications, 1989. Reflections on ecumenical prayer in our world community. A way to open up our theology in the humility of prayer.

Evely, Louis. *Teach Us How to Pray*. New York: Newman Press, 1967. Reflections on today's society at prayer. Rich and provocative.

Gallen, John, SJ, ed. *Christians at Prayer*. Notre Dame, IN: University of Notre Dame Press, 1977. Delightful essays by a variety of spiritual writers. The variety is valuable.

Hart, Thomas. *Spiritual Quest*. New York: Paulist Press, 1999. An excellent treatment for spirituality in a new cosmology. Poignant and revealing.

Kabat-Zinn, Jon. *Wherever You Go, There You Are*. New York: Hyperion, 1994. A full search of our human experience both East and West for more authentic reflective living. Meant to be reread.

Leech, Kenneth. *True Prayer: An Invitation to Christian Spirituality*. New York: Harper & Row, Publishers, 1980. Deeper and more cerebral reflections on the power of prayer.

Magee, John. *Reality and Prayer*. New York: Harper and Brothers, 1957. A clear scholarly treatment of the basic types of prayer using a range of examples from philosophy and theology.

Ne'Doncelle, Maurice. *God's Encounter with Man*. New York: Sheed & Ward, 1964. A literary approach to prayer using past cultures for our present experience.